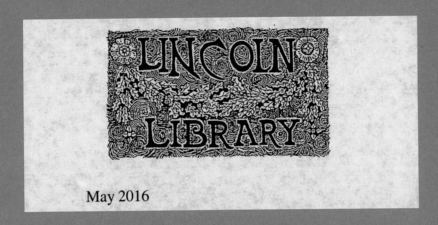

Rocky Mountain
National Park

PRESERVING AMERICA

Nate Frisch

Published by
CREATIVE EDUCATION AND CREATIVE PAPERBACKS

P.O. Box 227, Mankato, Minnesota 56002
Creative Education and Creative Paperbacks are imprints of The Creative Company
www.thecreativecompany.us

Design and production by Danny Nanos of Gilbert & Nanos
Art direction by Rita Marshall
Printed in Malaysia

Photographs by Alamy (Danita Delimont, Ed Endicott, Rolf Nussbaumer Photography, Jill Stephenson), Dreamstime (Bflorky, Jborzicchi, Puppie2008, Tupungato), Flickr (Marie Hitzemann), National Park Service, Shutterstock (AVprophoto, bjul, Zack C, Capture Light, cvm, Sharon Day, John De Bord, Robert Eastman, Jami Garrison, Arina P Habich, James BO Insogna, IrinaK, Eric Isselee, jtbaskinphoto, Alexey Kamenskiy, chris kolaczan, Yuriy Kulik, Robert Kyllo, David Osborn, paradoks_blizanaca, pashabo, David B. Petersen, Protasov AN, Tom Reichner, RIRF Stock, Phillip Rubino, Nelson Sirlin, South12th Photography, tristan tan, tjwvandongen, Tupungato, Sergey Uryadnikov, Krzysztof Wiktor)

Library of Congress Cataloging-in-Publication Data

Frisch, Nate.
Rocky Mountain National Park / Nate Frisch.
p. cm. — (Preserving America)
Includes bibliographical references and index.
Summary: An exploration of Rocky Mountain National Park, including how its mountainous landscape was formed,
its history of preservation, and tourist attractions such as the towering summit of Longs Peak.

ISBN 978-1-60818-607-5 (hardcover)
ISBN 978-1-62832-182-1 (pbk)
1. Rocky Mountain National Park (Colo.)—Juvenile literature. I. Title.
F782.R59F755 2015
978.8'69—dc23   2014028060

CCSS: RI.5.1, 2, 3, 8; RI.6.1, 2, 3, 4, 5, 6, 7; RH.6–8.4, 5, 6, 7, 8

First Edition HC 9 8 7 6 5 4 3 2 1
First Edition PBK 9 8 7 6 5 4 3 2 1

Cover & page 3: *Mills Lake, with view to Longs Peak; a bald eagle*

3/16 - Direct - $38.50

CREATIVE EDUCATION • CREATIVE PAPERBACKS

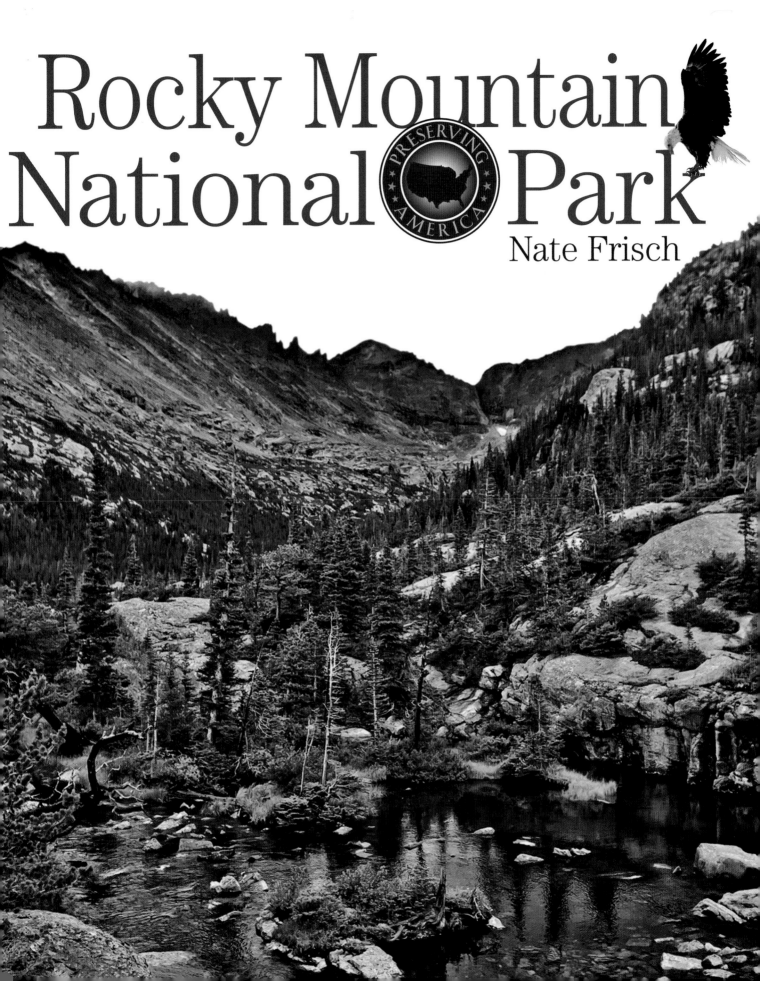

Rocky Mountain National Park

Nate Frisch

PRESERVING AMERICA

Table of Contents

TOWERING MOUNTAINS and glassy lakes. Churning rivers and dense forests. Lush prairies and baking deserts. The open spaces and natural wonders of the United States once seemed as limitless as they were diverse. But as human expansion and development increased in the 1800s, forests and prairies were replaced by settlements and agricultural lands. Waterways were diverted, wildlife was overhunted, and the earth was scarred by mining. Fortunately, many Americans fought to preserve some of the country's vanishing wilderness. In 1872, Yellowstone National Park was established, becoming the first true national park in the world and paving the way for future preservation efforts. In 1901, Theodore Roosevelt became U.S. president. He once stated, "There can be no greater issue than that of conservation in this country," and during his presidency, Roosevelt signed five national parks into existence. The National Park Service (NPS) was created in 1916 to manage the growing number of U.S. parks, including Rocky Mountain National Park in Colorado. For a century, the park has lured visitors up among the initially forbidding mountain peaks to discover a high-altitude world brimming with lush landscapes and vibrant life.

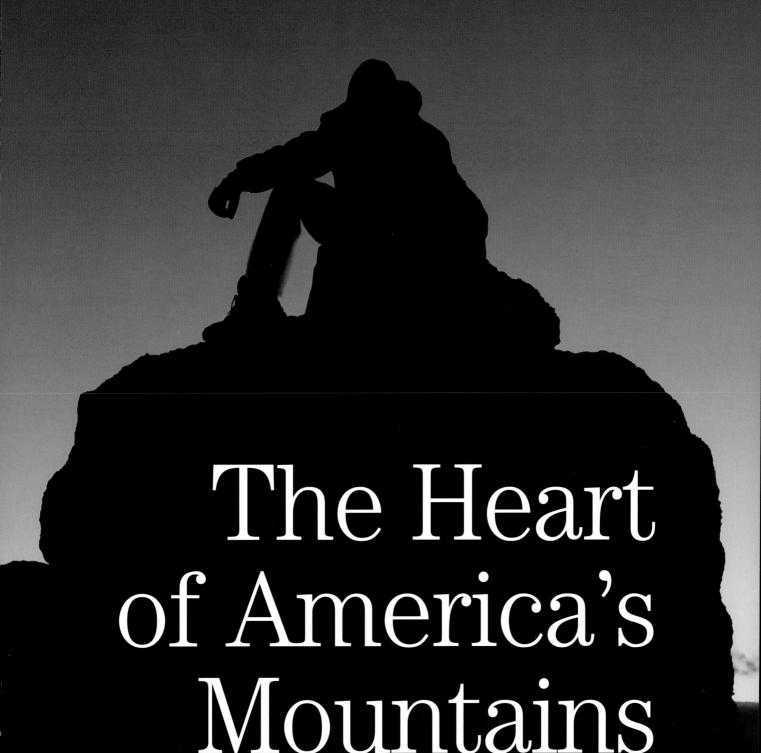

The Heart
of America's
Mountains

Rocky Mountain National Park—a park of this name could exist in any number of places. The Rocky Mountain Range stretches 3,000 miles (4,828 km) from southern New Mexico to northern British Columbia in Canada and spreads 300 miles (483 km) across in some places. But the highest, most forbidding peaks of the "Rockies" are found in Colorado. It seems most fitting that Rocky Mountain National Park should be found there as well.

Eighty million years ago, however, the name would not have been appropriate. At that time, much of the land was so low that it lay beneath a huge, shallow sea. Beneath the sandy seafloor were layers of granite—a rock that formed when molten rock called magma slowly cooled and solidified. As it cooled, the magma formed a structure of large, interlocking crystals. Such an arrangement makes granite extremely strong and rigid.

Then powerful forces within the earth strained the layers of ancient granite. The resilient rock would not bend, but eventually, the wrenching made it snap violently. Once this break, or fault, began, slabs of rock on opposite sides would sometimes buckle upward against one another. Other times, one slab would slide beneath another, wedging it up in a process called subduction. Still other times, the shifting rock would increase pressure deep within the earth, forcing magma toward the surface and creating volcanoes. Such events occurred along the extensive fault line for millions of years and were often accompanied by fierce earthquakes.

By about 55 million years ago, the general uplift of the Rockies was complete. In place of a seabed was a fractured mountain range thousands of feet above sea level. Although mountain-building processes slowed from that point on,

fragmented chunks of earth would continue to tilt, lift, and collapse over time, forming dozens of separate ranges and valleys. Among them were the Mummy Range, the Never Summer Mountains, and the Front Range. The last of these was still rising 10 million years ago and contains some of the very tallest peaks within the Rockies, reaching higher than 14,000 feet (4,267 m) in elevation.

Colorado's Rocky Mountain National Park features high-altitude peaks and sloping valleys, including Glacier Gorge (pictured).

With the mountain building complete, the next stage was mountain sculpting. This came by way of glaciers about 2 million years ago. That was the start of a **glacial period**, which meant snow wouldn't melt away, even in summer. As snow piled deeper on the mountain slopes, it compressed into ice under its own weight. And as the masses of ice grew to many tons, gravity pulled them down the rugged slopes, causing them to dislodge and drag rock as they went.

Very slowly, glaciers slid along the paths of least resistance—areas that were softer or a little lower than others. In this way, certain courses were scraped and dug out, while nearby areas of rock went untouched, resulting in U-shaped canyons and grooves down the mountainsides. Other byproducts of the glaciers were moraines and glacial lakes.

Moraines are piles of earth and rocks left at the bottom of slopes when glaciers melted. Glacial lakes were dug out by glaciers and later filled up by melting ice.

As the glacial period ended, plant and animal life became more abundant around the Front Range and in the Rockies as a whole. The number and type of life forms found in what would become Rocky Mountain National Park were determined largely by the interplay of elevation and climate. Temperatures in the Rockies tend to be 4 °F (2.2 °C) cooler for every 1,000 feet (305 m) of rise. Therefore, the future park's low point of 7,860 feet (2,396 m) would likely be about 25 °F (13.9 °C) warmer than the apex of Longs Peak—14,259 feet (4,346 m)—at any given time. Wind is stronger at the higher elevations as well.

The mountaintops also affect precipitation and sunlight. Weather systems generally move from west to east. Mountains are obstacles they must rise above. The air cools as it rises, and moisture often **condenses** and falls as rain or snow. By the time a weather system passes over high mountain peaks, it tends to be drier. For this reason, areas west of

mountain ranges are typically moister and sustain more vegetation than areas to the east. A north-south relationship comes into play with sunlight. South-facing mountain slopes receive a lot of direct sunlight, while north-facing slopes may be constantly shaded. This too affects moisture levels and plant growth.

Rocky Mountain National Park is divided into three separate **ecosystems** or zones based mostly on elevation, but precipitation and sunlight account for variations within those zones. From lowest elevation to highest, they are montane, subalpine, and alpine tundra. The montane ecosystem ranges from the park's lowest point up to about 9,500 feet (2,896 m) and is characterized by mostly **coniferous** forests containing ponderosa and lodgepole pines along with some fir and spruce. Where water is more abundant, groves of **deciduous** aspens, grassy meadows, and wildflowers are common, and willows and various bushes grow near lakes, ponds, and rivers.

The subalpine ecosystem begins near the higher reaches of the montane and extends to around 11,000 feet (3,353 m) above sea level.

The Rockies experience wide-ranging summer conditions, from thunderstorms (below) to melting snow (opposite).

High-elevation trees have adapted to the harsh weather, rocky soil, and generally dry conditions of the Rockies.

Here, pine tree growth tapers off and leafy trees are completely absent, leaving higher slopes to the fir and spruce trees. Even these fade out and look sickly as they approach the highest zone, the alpine tundra. This cold, windy ecosystem is devoid of trees and bushes. Only small, fast-growing grasses and plants sprout during the short growing season. Lichens, which are formed from **algae** living on fungi, cling to rocks year round.

These ecosystems also support a wide variety of animal life that cross between the zones, particularly as seasons change. Many animals—such as elk, mule deer, bighorn sheep, and mountain lions—move to higher elevations during the summer and descend to lower altitudes in the winter. Other animals, such as moose, black bears, and otters, prefer the lower elevations all year, while only American pikas and a few rodents tough out the mountaintops year round. Historically, the park area was also home to bison, grizzly bears, and wolves.

The region is currently home to 282 identified bird species. Among these are white-tailed ptarmigans—hardy grouse that inhabit the upper ecosystems and whose coloration changes with the seasons to provide camouflage. In the montane, the American dipper walks along stream bottoms to prey upon water insects and tiny fish. Various **raptors** and many songbirds also live in the region.

Cold-blooded reptiles and amphibians are less common in the cool climate of Rocky Mountain National Park. Three frog species, tiger salamanders, boreal toads, and western terrestrial garter snakes make up the entire roster. Eleven species of fish, including three types of cutthroat trout —named for the red coloring often present on their gill covers—live in the area's lakes, ponds, and streams.

The first evidence of human habitation in the region dates back to around 10,000 years ago. These Paleo-Indians likely came and went with the seasons, hunting big game and collecting vegetation during the summer, and then descending to lower elevations before the winter set in. Between A.D. 1200 and 1300, the Ute Indian tribe began settling in the region. They were followed by the Apache and Arapaho. All the tribes favored the area for its large game, which provided not only food but also hides, bones, horns, and other animal parts that were useful in making clothing, various tools, and decorations.

The insect-eating tiger salamander spends most of the year underground but requires a pond or other water to breed.

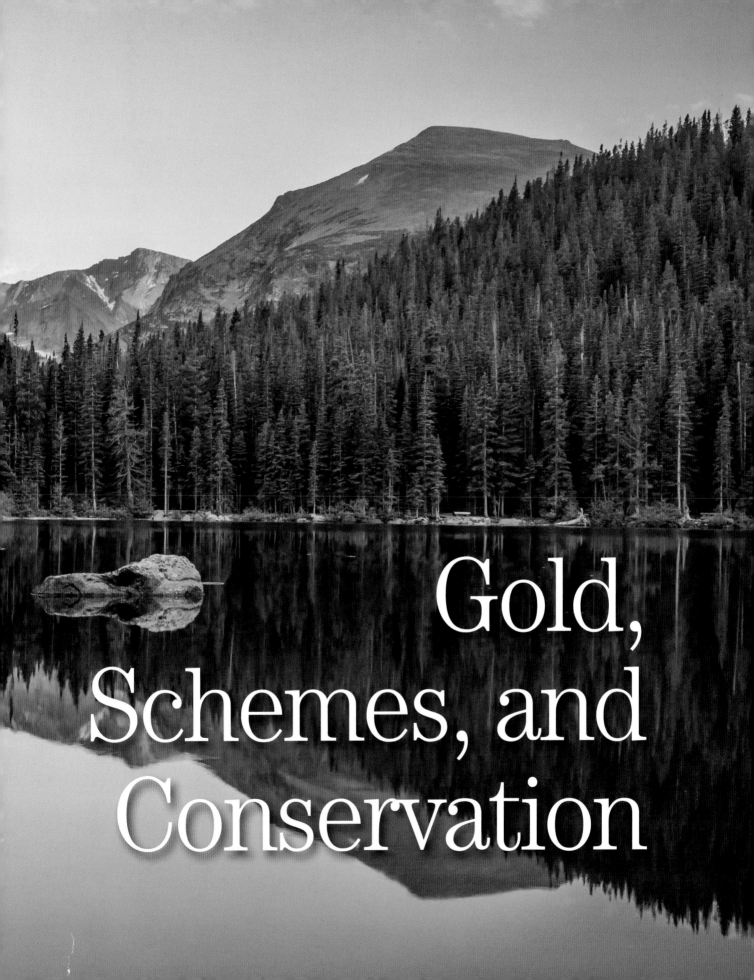

Gold,
Schemes, and
Conservation

The first Europeans to enter or pass near the Rocky Mountain National Park region were likely French fur trappers who reached the Rockies in the late 1700s. Beaver pelts were especially prized for their use in women's fashions of the day, and the numerous small lakes and streams in the area made for promising beaver habitat. As the pelts were sent back to the eastern U.S. for purchase, tales of the untamed region were relayed as well.

In 1803, the U.S. acquired territory in the Louisiana Purchase that stretched from the Mississippi River to the Rocky Mountains. The American government was eager to learn more about this uncharted land, and special exploration divisions of the army were created. One of the most influential explorers of the American plains and West was Major Stephen H. Long. Long was a brilliant engineer and personally designed the steamboat that would be used on his journeys up the Missouri and Platte river systems.

In 1820, the Platte brought Long and his crew near the area that would become Rocky Mountain National Park. Although the expedition mostly stayed on lower terrain east of the imposing Front Range, scientists documented their observations of the land, water, plants, and animals, while artists captured the sights in their paintings. The party named many landmarks in the area, including Longs Peak, the highest point of the future park. The crew also gained information about the region from different Indian tribes they met along their journey.

After skinning a beaver, trappers use wood or wire stretchers to dry the animal pelt before preparing it for sale.

When the expedition returned east, the Front Range was left in the hands of the Indians and fur trappers until the demand for furs died out in the early 1840s. A writer named Rufus B. Sage came to the Rockies in 1843, and, unlike Long's crew, he traveled into the very land that would become the park. His book *Scenes of the Rocky*

Mountains provided the first written accounts of the area.

Close on Sage's heels were thousands of hopeful prospectors who surged west looking for gold after 1848. Most were destined for California but tried their luck in the waterways of the Rocky Mountains. Success in the Rockies was slim until 1858, when 1.4 pounds (0.6 kg) of gold were found in a stream about 50 miles (80.5 km) southeast of the future park. The Pike's Peak Gold Rush had begun.

As the region became inundated with gold-seekers, **boom towns** such as Denver City and Boulder City sprang up, and prospectors spread far and wide. By 1861, the easily accessible gold supply had dried up. Although some commercial mining operations would remain, prospecting was no longer profitable for individuals. Many packed up and left, and small settlements became ghost towns.

Among those who stayed was a man named Joel Estes. Estes had discovered a meadow between the mountains east of the Front Range and decided to raise cattle there. Soon, other ranchers and homesteaders came to the meadow and founded the town of Estes Park.

The population boom created by the gold rush helped establish tourism and land management in the park region.

Today, the nearby city of Estes Park serves as a popular destination, featuring shops, restaurants, and hotels.

Ultimately, short growing seasons and long, harsh winters made agriculture difficult. But the area soon became increasingly valued for its scientific and tourist appeal. The 1860s and '70s brought more government-funded explorations—led by the likes of John Wesley Powell and Ferdinand Hayden—to the region. They scaled Longs Peak and other mountains, surveyed valleys and rivers, and studied the diverse flora and fauna (plant and animal life).

Stories of wild game attracted Windham Wyndham-Quin, an Irish entrepreneur and politician whose official title was the Earl of Dunraven. An avid hunter, he attempted to buy all the land of Estes Park for his own private game preserve in the early 1870s. What the wealthy earl couldn't buy outright he would sometimes gain through scheming and intimidation, and a couple landowners who refused to sell even died under mysterious circumstances. Although he bought most of the land, enough was retained by other settlers that his initial plan for a total takeover never worked out. So the earl built the three-story English Hotel to promote and profit from the increasing tourism industry.

At the same time, Abner E. Sprague—one of many people opposed to Wyndham-Quin's land grab—was developing his own tourist business. Unable to get land in Estes Park, Sprague built a home farther west in a valley called Moraine Park. He then created Sprague's Ranch, a **dude ranch** where visitors could get a taste of cowboy life. To visitors from parts of the eastern U.S., seeing the towering mountains, expansive pine forests, clear alpine lakes, and large, impressive wildlife was like visiting another world.

But the magnificent natural resources were valued for more than sightseeing in the late 1800s. Mining companies used destructive machines and explosives in their search for gold, silver, and other metals. Irrigation ditches were built along the Colorado River and other natural waterways in the mountains to divert water for agricultural use. Professional hunters eliminated entire populations of animals such as grizzly bears, wolves, bison, elk, and bighorn sheep. And the logging industry grew to support increasing populations in Colorado, which became a state in 1876.

Made a ghost town by the sudden decline of the mining industry, central Colorado's St. Elmo is now open to tourists.

*Known as the
"Father of the
National Parks,"
John Muir founded
the Sierra Club
in 1892.*

In 1886, the primary champion of Rocky Mountain National Park arrived in the form of the teenaged Enos Mills. The boy moved to Estes Park alone. Soon, he was scaling Longs Peak and exploring the forests, meadows, and wetlands. His love of mountains would lead him to investigate other ranges in the American West. While on a camping trip to California in 1889, Mills met John Muir, an eccentric but persuasive advocate of preservation. At that time, Muir was lobbying Congress for the creation of Yosemite National Park.

Muir inspired Mills, but it wasn't until a couple years later—after a trip to Wyoming's Yellowstone National Park—that Mills decided he would devote his efforts to establish a park in the Colorado Rockies. He moved back to Estes Park, where he operated Longs Peak Inn and guided tours through the mountain terrain and up Longs Peak. He advanced through various U.S. Forestry Service jobs, ultimately becoming a lecturer on forestry. And he wrote books and articles extolling the region's magnificence. Meanwhile, more development was creeping west from Estes Park into the areas Mills wanted protected.

Mills's efforts gained urgency. By the early 1900s, bison had already been wiped out of the region, and grizzly bears, wolves, elk, and bighorn sheep were nearly gone. Mills wrote hundreds of letters to politicians and frequently traveled to Washington, D.C., to lobby for a national park. Conservation groups such as Muir's Sierra Club stood behind his efforts, as did most of Colorado's nearby cities, which were eager for increased tourism opportunities.

Some opposition remained from the logging, mining, and agriculture industries, though, and their existing land claims and economic value forced Mills to ask for less land than he had originally desired. An industry that may have worked in Mills's favor, on the other hand, was that of automobiles. In the mid-1910s, more people were traveling farther and faster than ever before. This all but ensured tourism success for a scenic region that had long attracted visitors by horse-drawn stagecoach and wagon.

On January 26, 1915, president Woodrow Wilson signed the Rocky Mountain National Park Act, thus creating America's ninth national park. The 358-square-mile (927 sq km) park was somewhat rectangular but irregularly shaped because of the rivers and mountains that formed some of its borders. Although previous parks had featured mountainous scenery, none brought visitors up among the heights like Rocky Mountain National Park.

Generations of park visitors have traveled from near and far to take in Rocky Mountain's one-of-a-kind landscape.

Amusement Park or Natural Preserve?

When the park opened in 1915, its borders were still dotted with private lands. Many of the landowners had operated lodges before the park was established and continued to do so afterward. Moraine Park was especially populated with private businesses. Among them was the old Sprague's Ranch—revamped and renamed Stead's Ranch by this time. It boasted a golf course in addition to a swimming pool, a riding stable, rodeo grounds, and various lodgings.

The fledgling park, meanwhile, had more trouble getting up and running. Initially, the staff consisted of only three rangers, and they were allotted a small annual budget. Not only did they struggle to provide adequate guest facilities and services, but they also had difficulty monitoring illegal hunting, livestock grazing, and timber use.

Around this time, the last grizzlies and wolves in the area were killed. Surprisingly, even many conservationists believed this to be a good thing. Conventional thinking at the time suggested that eliminating predators benefited prey such as deer and elk. This may have been true in the short term, but over time, ecosystems became unbalanced. Certain animal populations grew too large, and limited space and food led to disease and starvation.

General management efforts of Rocky Mountain National Park improved moderately when the NPS was created in 1916. This new

Each winter, herds of 600 to 800 elk (below) inhabit the wild and mountainous terrain of the park (opposite).

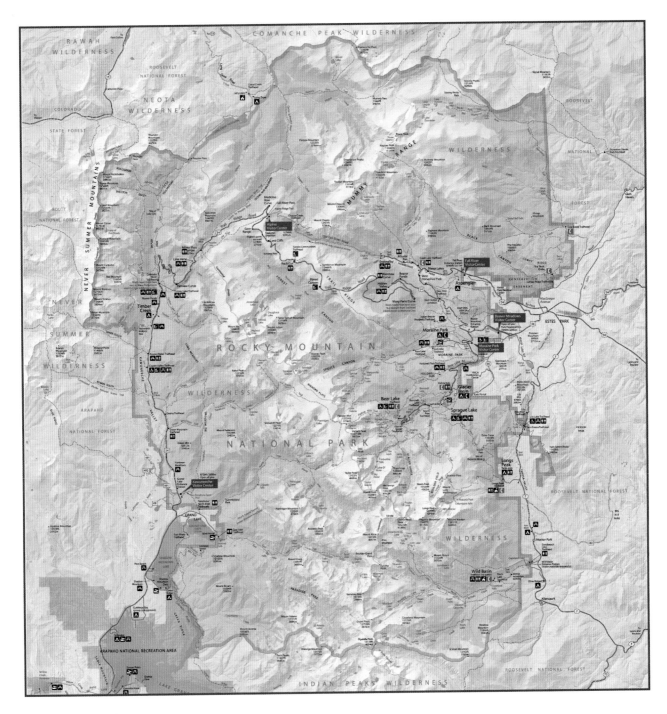

branch of the U.S. Department of the Interior focused specifically on
maintaining the natural appeal of national parks while also making them
accessible and welcoming to visitors. It established park rules and
development plans that were previously lacking in Rocky Mountain.
However, not everyone appreciated the creation and intervention of the

The older, one-way section of Rocky Mountain's Fall River Road was closed from 2013 to 2015 for flood repair.

NPS. Many Estes Park residents had assumed that decisions regarding park operations would be made by local committees, not by government workers in Washington. When the NPS began selecting **concessionaires** to provide services and transportation in the park, many locals working in the same trades were put out of business.

Some of the park's early marketing attempts were also questionable. One campaign touted the park as a new "Garden of Eden," and a young woman named Agnes Lowe was hired to play Eve. She wore a leopard-skin outfit, and media and visitors would watch as she ran through the meadows, ducked in and out of the woods, and attempted to snatch trout from the streams. In truth, while the park was publicizing her "survival" story, it was also putting her up in a lodge with good meals and a bed every night. The charade didn't sit well with some park rangers, who felt they should be promoting the park's natural attractions instead.

To enable increased traffic to flow through the new park, inmates of Colorado prisons constructed the Fall River Road. Completed in 1920, the road was noteworthy in that it led over the Front Range, connecting the busier eastern section of the park to the more remote western region. The challenging construction feat was all the more impressive, considering it was accomplished using hand shovels and picks. However, the dirt "motor trail" was narrow, steep, and generally treacherous.

Rocky Mountain did not remain its original size for long. The NPS gradually increased the total acreage by buying up private plots within the park's boundaries or by expanding the boundaries themselves. The

largest single expansion was the inclusion of the Never Summer Range in 1929. This scenic addition of mountains that feature patches of snow year round brought the park's size close to the 415 square miles (1,075 sq km) it covers today.

Winds blow fiercely at the highest elevations, with gusts at Longs Peak (above, far left) topping 70 miles (113 km) per hour.

With the 1930s came the Great Depression, a time when many Americans were poor and unemployed. In response, president Franklin D. Roosevelt created the Civilian Conservation Corps (CCC). The CCC hired single young men to perform manual labor on public lands throughout the country. In addition to constructing and remodeling buildings, grooming hiking trails, and managing fires in Rocky Mountain, the CCC was responsible for constructing the 48-mile (77.2 km) Trail Ridge Road. This improved an existing stretch of the Fall River Road and then split off to create a more gradual and scenic route over the Front Range. The route peaked at 12,183 feet (3,713 m) above sea level before leading down to the southwest corner of the park near the small town of Grand Lake. The winding path over the mountaintops remains a highlight of the park today, and the CCC-built Alpine Visitor Center near the route's highest point is still used in the summer.

A downhill ski area was also developed along the Trail Ridge Road, complete with lifts and warming houses. Some people opposed the ski area, claiming that it contradicted the park's purpose as a natural preserve and attraction. The ski area would operate for more than half a century but ultimately was closed in 1992, and the facilities were removed in 2002.

The 1940s were a slow time for national parks. The U.S. joined

Visitors inclined to cast a line (below) might reel in a rainbow trout (opposite), which average eight pounds (3.6 kg).

World War II, families weren't taking many vacations, and the government was more concerned with war efforts than with maintaining national park services and facilities. The 1950s and early '60s saw returning interest in national parks, but the focus was more on recreational aspects than on preservation. To comply with this trend, the NPS began modernizing parks with more lodges, visitor centers, and paved roads. Rocky Mountain did build roads and bridges and create the Beaver Meadows Entrance and Visitor Center, but, unlike many other parks, it did not add lodges.

Conservationism saw a resurgence beginning in the late '60s. Remaining private lands and businesses within the park were bought up and restored to natural conditions. The park set stricter rules about where visitors could drive and hike and made a greater effort to educate guests about the impact of their actions. Rocky Mountain also ended the long-practiced stocking of nonnative trout in park lakes and rivers. The stocking had begun to boost fishing and attract anglers, but introduced fish were squeezing out rarer native greenback cutthroat and Colorado River cutthroat. Since 1970, only native fish have been stocked in the park, and fishing regulations have promoted the reduction of nonnative populations.

The '70s also saw the introduction of moose. While these large deer may have wandered near the park in decades or centuries past, they probably never lived there in sustainable numbers. In 1978 and '79, 24 moose were released near the Never Summer Range. Within a few years, the population was breeding and had found its niche in the Kawuneeche Valley, which follows the Colorado River from the Grand Lake Entrance

up to the Never Summer Mountains. These impressive animals—the largest in the park—still call the valley home.

Fire has always been a concern in forested national parks, and for decades, policies of most parks dictated that any forest fires should be squelched immediately. This allowed more trees to grow taller, but as forests became densely packed, competition for sun, water, and soil made individual trees less healthy. And fallen trees and branches piled up on the forest floors. It was in the late 1980s that the drawbacks of this practice began to show. Uncontrollable fires ravaged Yellowstone National Park during a dry 1988 summer. Although this was many miles away from Rocky Mountain, it was a glimpse of what could happen if forest overcrowding was allowed to continue.

Also, an insect called the mountain pine beetle has lived in the Rockies since before humans arrived, but it became a serious issue only after pine forests grew too dense. This allowed the beetles to spread and multiply rapidly, and as their larvae fed on the trees' needles, the crowded trees became too unhealthy to withstand them. Today, large stands of brown pines are seen throughout the park. These dry trees add to the threat of unmanageable fires.

Since the early 2000s, Rocky Mountain officials have conducted more **prescribed burns**, believing that burning off small sections of forest under controlled conditions would reduce the danger and intensity of accidental fires later on. This is also one method of curbing the destruction of pine beetles.

In 2009, nearly 94 percent of Rocky Mountain was set apart as wilderness area. This designation forbade construction of roads, buildings, or any other facilities within the area's boundaries, ensuring that Rocky Mountain National Park will remain almost entirely untouched by human structures for many years to come.

Keeping Nature in the Spotlight

Rocky Mountain National Park receives about 3 million visitors per year and ranks among the nation's busiest parks in the summer. Contributing to its high attendance is its close proximity to Denver and other populous cities in eastern Colorado. The park is a convenient getaway for residents of these areas, and Denver, being the largest city within hundreds of miles, also attracts a number of rural visitors who may drive an extra 90 minutes to reach Rocky Mountain. Because many guests live nearby or view the park as a single stop on a busy itinerary, most visits are limited to a weekend or even one day.

Summer is the busiest time in the park. July and August yield the warmest temperatures, often peaking around 75 °F (23.9 °C) at lower altitudes. Higher elevations are colder, and mountaintops may receive snow at any time of year. Midday showers or storms are common in summer. Autumn tends to have less rain, making for firm hiking trails and drier camping, but nighttime temps often drop below freezing. Spring boasts forceful waterfalls and lush new plant growth, but the water runoff from the mountains makes some trails and roads impassable. Winter visitors are restricted to one half of the park or the other because the higher stretches of Trail Ridge Road are closed from late fall into the following spring.

Hikers often rest near the spray of Glacier Creek's Alberta Falls, named for Abner E. Sprague's wife.

When roads are open, driving is one of the most popular ways to experience the park. The Trail Ridge Road features switchbacks and winds along mountain ridges, but it basically follows an arc from Estes Park in the east to the Grand Lake Entrance in the west. This road offers a good sampling of the park's various terrains and ecosystems. Meadows and brisk streams at the east end shift to forests and then alpine tundra as motorists climb in elevation. Deer

are common in the lower elevations, bighorn sheep are present near the aptly named Sheep Lake, pikas are often seen highest up, and elk may be spotted anywhere. To the west, the road descends into the lush Kawuneeche Valley, where the Colorado River and surrounding wetlands make for good moose habitat. Trail Ridge Road has frequent pull-offs and overlooks as well as restrooms, picnic areas, and **trailheads**. It also passes by the Alpine Visitor Center, which sits nearly 12,000 feet (3,658 m) above sea level and features a ranger-staffed information desk, observation decks, a gift shop, and a restaurant.

Rocky Mountain has few other roads. Bear Lake Road begins near the Beaver Meadows Entrance and winds south past the Moraine Park

The Alpine Visitor Center at Fall River Pass (below) offers a scenic stop-off for both drivers and hikers (opposite).

Museum, a couple campgrounds, and several trailheads to reach Bear Lake. A spur off the Trail Ridge Road leads to the Alluvial Fan, an area featuring broad, sloping deposits of sediment over which water rushes down. Continuing on this route leads to the Old Fall River Road—a section of the old road that spanned the mountains. The narrow path serves as a one-way alternate route up to the Alpine Visitor Center. Accessing some other points in the park, such as the Longs Peak trailhead or the Wild Basin Area, requires motorists to use roads outside the park and then follow short routes back in.

While sightseeing from the roads offers many scenic vistas, hiking may be the best way to thoroughly appreciate the park. Rocky Mountain boasts about 350 miles (563 km) of hiking trails that range from short, easy strolls to strenuous treks over steep terrain. Most of the trails are at lower elevations, where interconnecting loops allow hikers to match their routes according to their fitness level, time allotment, and preference of scenery. Trails are especially dense between the Fall River Visitor Center and Bear Lake. Bear Lake is likely the busiest hiking area in the park, and shuttles run along Bear Lake Road to take visitors to the scenic lake and nearby trailheads. In addition to loops around various small lakes,

Rocky Mountain provides outdoor adventure for many interests, from rock climbing (pictured) to horseback riding (opposite).

popular short hikes lead to cascading waterfalls such as Adams Falls and Alberta Falls.

Higher-elevation trails are typically longer and more isolated. Especially high hikes or climbs, such as those up to Longs Peak, are not advised for casual or novice hikers. But lower, shorter hikes up summits such as Deer Mountain or Twin Sisters Peak—round-trip distances of 6 and 7.5 miles (9.7 and 12.1 km) respectively—also offer impressive views. Regardless of elevation, hikers wanting to reach the most remote areas of the park or spend more time out in nature have more than 500 **backcountry** campsites from which to choose. Whether guests make long treks or quick day hikes, they are generally told to stay on groomed trails, as wandering off the paths can damage plant life that the park is trying to protect or restore.

Horseback riders are permitted on about 80 percent of the park's total trail length. Exceptions include shorter, busier paths, such as those around Bear Lake. Many of the backcountry campsites accommodate horses overnight. For guests who don't bring or own a horse, various riding stables in or just outside the park offer guided rides ranging from an hour to multiple days.

With so many granite slopes available, mountain climbing is another popular activity in the park. No special permit is required, but climbers must follow rules that minimize damage to the rock. For novice climbers or those without their own gear, concessionaires can provide equipment, lessons, and supervision.

Rocky Mountain National Park contains 156 small lakes and many streams. Park officials believe 48 of the lakes contain self-sustaining populations of trout or other fish. Some of these, such as Bear Lake, are not open to fishing. Others allow catch-and-release only. Among the

Conservation efforts throughout North America have restored populations of bighorn sheep to native habitats.

most accessible catch-and-keep lakes are Sprague in the eastern part of the park and Poudre in the west. Anglers older than 15 must have a Colorado fishing license, and only artificial lures may be used. Non-motorized watercraft are allowed on all lakes except Bear Lake.

Winter visitors get to experience snowy scenery and small crowds. They may be limited to lower elevations (because of road closures), but this is where most wildlife gathers, too. Winter can be the best time to spot animals against the white backdrop of snow. Winter activities include sledding or tubing at the former Hidden Valley ski area, snowshoeing on most of the park trails, and cross-country skiing throughout the park.

Guests spending more than a day in Rocky Mountain during warmer months may stay at one of the five campgrounds available. There are more than 550 sites within these campgrounds. The two largest, Moraine Park and Glacier Basin, also have group campsites. Along with Aspenglen, they take reservations, while Longs Peak and

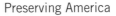

Timber Creek work on a first-come, first-served basis. Longs Peak is the smallest and most primitive campground. It does not allow RVs and has only outhouse-type toilets. The others feature running water and flush toilets during warmer months, but none has RV hookups or electricity. All sites feature picnic tables and fire rings, and bear-proof food lockers are available throughout the campgrounds. Visitors wanting plusher accommodations have many hotel options in Estes Park and, to a lesser extent, in Grand Lake.

From a park that once struggled to find a balance between preservation and tourist entertainment, Rocky Mountain has established itself as one of the more natural parks in the U.S. Limited roads, protective hiking guidelines, and even the lack of lodging ensure that emphasis remains on the attractions that existed long before people arrived. Today, the imposing, rugged mountainscapes still call to distant travelers, and when they arrive, they are captivated by the intricate details of the mountain streams, meadows, lakes, forests, and wildlife. In this way, Rocky Mountain National Park demonstrates that preservation in America is as much about sheltering the smallest birds and flowers as it is about protecting the grandest mountains.

The broad-tailed hummingbird makes its summer home in the high elevations of Rocky Mountain National Park.

Rocky Mountain Battering Rams

The most iconic animal of American mountains is likely the bighorn sheep. Split hooves with ridged bottoms allow the stocky animals to navigate the steepest terrains with ease. Both sexes grow horns, but only the males develop the massive curls that can weigh up to 30 pounds (13.6 kg) per set. The rams use these in explosive head-to-head battles for mating rights. Aside from mating season, rams and ewes live apart, with the males forming small bachelor groups and the females maintaining larger groups with their young. Bighorn sheep graze on coarse grasses and plants and typically move to lower elevations in winter to feed.

Big Mountains, Small Residents

Although pikas resemble large mice, these hardy mountain-dwellers are more closely related to rabbits. American pikas do not dig burrows but rather inhabit naturally protective shelters such as rock piles. Here, they can hide from predators such as hawks, coyotes, and bobcats. They spend their summer days foraging for grasses, seeds, and nearly any

plant available. They stockpile food in their shelter to last through the snowy winter. Like rabbits, pikas will consume their food twice—eating their own droppings after the initial meal to take in remaining nutrients.

A Hidden Hiking Hub

Tucked 15 miles (24.1 km) south of the Beaver Meadows Entrance is the Wild Basin Entrance. This isolated area contains three trailheads, a picnic area, and restrooms. The 30 miles (48.3 km) of trail here do not connect to any others in the park and feature their own lakes and waterfalls.

Hikers starting from the Wild Basin Trailhead can hit Copeland, Calypso, and Ouzel falls all along a single 2.7-mile (4.3 km) route. Continuing onward and upward would yield picturesque, mountain-rimmed lakes, including Ouzel, Bluebird, Thunder, and Lion. Add backcountry campsites, and the Wild Basin Area can be a side trip or the centerpiece of a Rocky Mountain visit.

Seeking Greener Pastures

While most people come to Rocky Mountain National Park to see the mountains, the lush valleys within the park can be captivating in their own right. The abundant food sources also attract impressive wildlife.

The Timber Lake Trail in the northwestern area of the park is among the best for reaching these vibrant meadows. Hikers could follow it all the way to the sloping green shores of Timber Lake, but they might prefer splitting off onto Long Meadows Trail, which offers some of the best chances to see black bear and moose as well as the more common deer and elk.

Boating in the Mountains

Rocky Mountain National Park has numerous small, scenic lakes that are well suited for short hiking loops, casual fishing, and leisurely canoe or kayak paddling. But guests wanting to use bigger or faster boats or spend longer periods offshore might want to visit the Arapaho National Recreation Area right along the park's southwestern border. The area contains five reservoirs, the largest of which are Lake Granby (pictured) and Shadow Mountain Lake. Both allow motorboats and are stocked with fish—Granby with lake trout and kokanee salmon; Shadow Mountain with various trout species. Marinas rent out various types of watercraft as well as waterskiing and tubing equipment.

Experiencing Nature Indoors

Visitors to national parks are typically interested in nature and often appreciate knowledge of history and science as well. For such guests, the

Denver Museum of Nature and Science would be appealing. The three-story museum features permanent exhibits of many types of animals and ecosystems from around the world, plus fossils and reconstructions of dinosaurs and prehistoric mammals that once inhabited the area. Other exhibits present American Indian information and artifacts, mineral and gem collections, and various non-regional topics. Regularly changing temporary exhibits and films in its theaters helps the museum appeal to a wide range of ages and interests.

Breathtaking Peaks

The highest point in Rocky Mountain National Park is 14,259 feet (4,346 m) above sea level, and the lowest is still high by some standards—7,860 feet (2,396 m). Because the air is less dense and contains less oxygen at higher elevations, visitors unused to these heights typically experience shortness of breath. They may also suffer from headaches, dizziness, nausea, and loss of coordination. Lowlanders are advised to spend a day or two at around 8,000 feet (2,438 m) before attempting physical activity in higher reaches of the park. Those venturing into higher elevations should also take in extra fluids and calories.

Hidden Threats

From spring to midsummer, Rocky Mountain wood ticks climb onto leaves or grass and grab hold of mammals—including humans—that pass by. They then latch onto skin and bite into their host. A small percentage of these parasites carry diseases such as Colorado tick fever, which can cause headaches, nausea, vomiting, weakness, body pain, and rashes for about one to three weeks. No specific treatment for the illness exists, so prevention is key. Hikers should use insect repellent

and wear long pants, socks, and sleeves—tucking layers into one another. And anyone who's been outside should periodically inspect their clothing and skin for ticks.

Glossary

algae: tiny plantlike organisms that lack the leaves, stems, and roots of true plants

backcountry: an area that is away from developed or populated areas

boom towns: communities that spring up or expand rapidly as a result of a surge, or "boom," in the local economy

concessionaires: people or organizations operating businesses on sites owned by someone else

condenses: changes from a gas or vapor into a liquid

coniferous: describing plants that usually have needle-shaped or scale-like leaves and seed-producing cones

deciduous: describing plants that shed their leaves in the fall

dude ranch: a ranch operated primarily as a vacation resort, typically catering to clients with minimal knowledge of ranch operations

ecosystems: communities of animals, plants, and other living things interacting together within an environment

glacial period: any period in history when ice covered much of the earth

prescribed burns: fires that are intentionally ignited and contained within a designated area as a means of reducing fire hazards or promoting new plant growth

raptors: birds of prey such as hawks, owls, eagles, and vultures

trailheads: the starting points of walking or hiking trails

Selected Bibliography

Emerick, John C. *Rocky Mountain National Park Natural History Handbook*. Boulder, Colo.: Roberts Rinehart, 1994.

Laine, Don, Barbara Laine, Jack Olson, Eric Peterson, and Shane Christensen. *Frommer's National Parks of the American West*. Hoboken, N.J.: Wiley, 2010.

Malitz, Jerome. *Rocky Mountain National Park Dayhiker's Guide*. Boulder, Colo.: Johnson Books, 1993.

National Geographic Guide to the National Parks of the United States. Washington, D.C.: National Geographic, 2009.

Schullery, Paul. *America's National Parks: The Spectacular Forces That Shaped Our Treasured Lands*. New York: DK, 2001.

White, Mel. *Complete National Parks of the United States*. Washington, D.C.: National Geographic, 2009.

Websites

National Geographic: Rocky Mountain National Park
http://travel.nationalgeographic.com/travel/national-parks
/rocky-mountain-national-park
This site provides a concise visitor's guide to the park, complete with maps, photos, sightseeing suggestions, and links to other popular national parks.

Rocky Mountain National Park
http://www.nps.gov/romo/index.htm
The official National Park Service site for Rocky Mountain is the most complete online source for information on the park and includes tips for park sightseeing, activities, and safety. Park regulations, lodging information, and various maps are also provided.

Note: *Every effort has been made to ensure that the websites listed above are suitable for children, that they have educational value, and that they contain no inappropriate material. However, because of the nature of the Internet, it is impossible to guarantee that these sites will remain active indefinitely or that their contents will not be altered.*

Index